# CLOSING THE ACHIEVEMENT GAP

# CLOSING THE ACHIEVEMENT GAP

Reaching and Teaching High Poverty Learners:

101 Top Strategies
to Help High Poverty Learners Succeed

*Written by: Tiffany Chane'l Anderson*

iUniverse, Inc.
New York  Lincoln  Shanghai

Closing the Achievement Gap
Reaching and Teaching High Poverty Learners:
101 Top Strategies to Help High Poverty Learners Succeed

Copyright © 2004, 2007 by Tiffany Anderson

iUniverse books may be ordered through booksellers or by contacting:

iUniverse
2021 Pine Lake Road, Suite 100
Lincoln, NE 68512
www.iuniverse.com
1-800-Authors (1-800-288-4677)

ISBN: 978-0-595-33478-0 (pbk)
ISBN: 978-0-595-78274-1 (ebk)

Printed in the United States of America

# CONTENTS

# ACKNOWLEDGMENTS

First and foremost, I thank God for blessing me with the talent to teach, as my steps are ordered by the Lord.

Teaching is a ministry in its own category. It is written in Matthew 18:12–14:

> How think ye? If a man have a hundred sheep, and one of them is gone astray, doth not he leave the ninety and nine, and goeth into the mountains, and seeketh that which is gone astray? And if so be that he find it, verily I say unto you, he rejoiceth more of that sheep, than that of the ninety and nine which went not astray. Even so it is not the will of your Father which is in heaven, that one of these little ones should perish.

While God has led my spiritual life, there have been many teachers in my physical life who have taught me the importance of education. These teachers include (but are not limited to) the great black leaders who came before my time. I have learned so much from reading their literature, poetry, and stories of black activism. I thank my parents, who both had early careers in teaching and life-long careers in ministry. They completed their graduate educations in seminary and raised me in a Baptist church. My most important students and teachers are those within my own home: my husband, Stanley, and my two children, Whitney and Christopher.

They are my support system; they encourage me to touch as many lives through teaching as I can. Lastly ... at the end of a person's formal schooling, there is often one educator who stands out, one who has demonstrated unconditional love and support. For me, this was my fifth-grade teacher at Jackson Park in University City, Missouri: Ms. Green, who inspired me to stand out from the crowd and to be proud of my gifts and talents.

I thank all of these individuals for giving me the resources that have helped me to grow into the teacher I am today. The strategies found within this text have been compiled both from the teachers and schools that have so willingly allowed me to observe them, and from my own experience of having seen and documented what works in the classroom. Too often, we look at what doesn't work in educational pedagogy—more time needs to be spent studying success stories and positive strategies, which can teach us far more.

# INTRODUCTION

The national gap between black and white achievement in education has recently become a greater concern for all districts—suburban, urban, and rural—as they all face sanctions under the No Child Left Behind Act if subgroups of children (often minority children) continue to be left behind. While this book does not attempt either to advocate or to point out the problems (such as lack of funding) with the No Child Left Behind Act (Public Law 107–110), it does recognize that greater national attention has been focused on the gap as a result of the act. This gap, however, is not a new phenomenon—it is an ongoing issue that has previously been ignored nationally. While there are many sections of the act that address many more issues aside from sanctions for schools that receive federal funds and do not meet annual performance standards, the No Child Left Behind Act has changed the focus for schools across the nation. Many schools that were once considered "high-performing" are now seen as in need of improvement under the provisions of the act. Interested readers can review the full act—which is over 600 pages long—at the U.S. Department of Education's Web site at www.ed.gov.

While the act is new, the black-white gap has been a longstanding problem. The education of black students in high-poverty settings has continued to be inferior, and full access to equal educational opportunities has yet to occur. Schools that boldly step out of the box and provide all children with equal access to challenging curricula, while also giving them value and a sense of cultural competency, will outperform schools that succumb to the achievement-gap syndrome. Building cultural competency in schools will ultimately require better education for teachers at the college level; until that occurs, schools must take charge in educating their teachers about how they can better instruct their students. Eliminating the achievement gap as it relates to racism and poverty is complex in that the problem's solutions must challenge the fabric from which this nation is built. For example, educators should not start teaching "black history" with the Atlantic Slave Trade, but with the history that begins long before that and includes African civilizations, kings, and queens.

While many may disagree with the No Child Left Behind Act, its sanctions are economic ones, and economics is the engine that has historically and continues to drive our nation.

The ramifications of economics are the force behind racism, educational reform, and national policies. Lack of wealth often equals less educational access. Poverty is intertwined with the achievement gap. Schools are separated by socioeconomic class just as much as by race. In single-race schools, poor students score lower than upper-middle-class students. Racism and the inequities caused by "economic privilege" remain diseases that our nation has not adequately confronted. They are the underlying cause of disparities in black-white housing patterns, unequal access to higher education, higher black incarceration rates, and even differences in income between similar job categories for whites and blacks. The strategies suggested in this book focus on enabling teachers to better reach high-poverty learners. These strategies will empower educators to help students move out of the cycle of poverty.

We will be focusing on the black-white gap, given that this is the largest gap and that blacks constitute the second-largest population in the United States. It is important to note the poverty rate among blacks. According to the U.S. Census in 2003, the African American poverty rate is 24.4 percent, and the highest numbers of people in poverty are children. The poverty rate in 2003 had increased from that of previous years. As poverty increases, the issues surrounding the achievement gap continue to grow in importance as well. There are thirty-six million African American people (12 percent of the United States population), and the following are some startling facts about them from the 2003 U.S. Census and from the Journal of Blacks in Higher Education:

- 33 percent of African Americans are under the age of eighteen.

- The poverty rate for African Americans is 24 percent, and that of whites is 8 percent.

- More black men are in prison than in college.

These few facts are simple illustrations of the link between poverty and the achievement gap. Generational poverty, low college entry, and higher numbers in correctional institutions each play a role in a kind of snowball effect that tends to make existing problems even worse. While poverty is not the only link, it will be the focus of this book. Educators must first confront the fact that poverty is an issue that must be addressed, and they must understand that poverty is no excuse for standards to be lowered. To lower educational standards because of a student's poverty would serve only to perpetuate a vicious cycle and widen further the achievement gaps that he or she faces.

When poverty is overlooked and educators become "color-blind" to issues of class and race—which are very real for the people within the subgroups—they often fail to educate. Education with support is what is needed, not the lowering of expectations as the support to fit the subgroup. When educators lower their expectations, children are stripped of tools they might have worked with or defended themselves with. Therefore, the following chapters will concentrate on instructional strategies that work for high-poverty learners without reducing the expectation of positive results.

The economic gap does overlap with that of race, and, without quality educational opportunities being afforded to children, the economic gap becomes a generational cycle. The rate of black men living in poverty is 20 percent—three times that of white men, which is 7 percent. The poverty rate for black women is 25 percent—twice that of white women, which is 9 percent. For men and women over the age of sixty-five, black men and women live in poverty at a rate that is three times higher than that for whites. There are thirty-two million people living in poverty in the United States—this is 12 percent of the population, representing eight million blacks and fifteen million whites, according to the 2003 U.S. Census.

As the economic gap widens along racial lines, a related effect can be seen in the incarceration rate. There are 4,834 black male prisoners for every 100,000 black males in the United States, compared to 680 white males in prison for every 100,000 white males. Out of the 2,078,570 male prisoners in the United States, 757,000 are black, according to the Autumn 2003 issue of the Journal of Blacks in Higher Education. In 1990, there were 609,690 black men in prison, which was greater than the number (436,000) of all black men enrolled in college, and this disparity persists today. Clearly, the economic gap exacerbates the black-white achievement gap, and it is dangerously packaged in the box of racism and classism.

The following list contains 101 strategies that have been seen to move students rapidly in a positive direction. Much like medicine, education is a science that calls for the analysis of data and for treatment based on diagnoses. Even as these strategies are implemented, data must continue to be analyzed to ensure that students continue to grow and develop to their full potential. The 101 strategies, all carefully selected, have been chosen because they are reflective of specific techniques that great educators have used to inspire, motivate, and instruct children whom some may have considered too poor to learn. In order for teachers to succeed, the correct positive construct must be held. Educators must understand their power to create optimum learning environments, their power to turn a life around, and their power to teach those whom others could not. It is this self-efficacy that will determine how well one teaches.

Whereas medical doctors recognize their power because they can see the external ramifications of their failures, teachers can have difficulty understanding their power because the "death" of a student occurs internally—the child's external reactions are the manifestations of the fractures of the mind within. If teachers could see the internal chemical changes within their students' minds—the dendrites growing as a concept is taught, the switches of understanding being thrown—they would appreciate their own powers much more. In addition, if they could see the shutting down of students' internal systems when they lack positive feedback, they would better understand their power to change a life as well. A doctor's effectiveness is predicted by three things he or she must do:

(1) Know the patient. Educators must know their students.

(2) Understand the power they have to change conditions. Teachers must be aware of the power of their position.

(3) Use data to diagnose, to implement strategies, and to follow progress closely. Teachers must be data-driven as well. Based on data implement strategies, and follow progress.

While keeping these three things in mind, you must realize that a strategy that works for one student might not work for another. Without knowing you or your students' data, I cannot prescribe the particular strategies you should use. However, I can state that the strategies I present in this book do positively affect high-poverty learners and can make the ultimate difference in a school's improvement. Among the 101 strategies listed, there will be some that you have never used before that will work well for you. There will also be some that you cannot use because of the dynamics of your classroom or school. I encourage you to try what you can from the list and pass on strategies to other educators to try. By doing this, we can educate and empower one another.

Many times, we know that we are working hard, but, because we are not working hard at the missing links, we see no change. It is my hope that we, as educators, will work hard at identifying the missing links and implement strategies to make those links strong for children to better make connections. Education is the only profession that is the foundation for every other profession. Education is the key to knowledge. A teacher will touch the lives of the world's future professionals. It is because of this power that teachers take on the role of missionaries. They are often underpaid and undervalued by those outside the organization. However, they save more lives than any other profession, resulting in a priceless reward of knowledge. I challenge every educator to use your power to reach and teach each child! If you succeed in doing this, much like a missionary, the lives you can save will be countless!

# Chapter 1

# Building Relationships

In most educational research on leadership styles and school climate, relationship-building is a key factor. Teachers are leaders in their classrooms, and, in order for significant learning to occur in any class or in any school, relationships must be built. Steven Covey describes the effect relationships have on production and production capability by stating, "You see it when you really take time to invest in a relationship and you find the desire and ability to work together and communicate takes a quantum leap." (Covey 1989)

Strategies

1. Make home visits; be visible in the neighborhood and in the school.

2. Use culturally relevant material from the student's environment within lessons in order to personalize them.

3. Talk to your students and their families. Identify the neediest students and student leaders who are high-poverty, and schedule a book talk,

luncheon, or interview with them in order to find out what helps them learn, and what aspects of school they like.

4.   Help students get to know you by weaving stories about your life into class lessons.

5.   Discuss current events and ask students what they think about societal issues.

6.   Create opportunities for staff and students to conduct dialogues. Often, staff meetings are used for school-management business. There is great power in constructive, problem-solving dialogue. A possible topic might be, "What are your thoughts on difficult students? How should we define them, and what strategies should we use to help them?" Allow staff to discuss the topic. Such conversations will bring out staff or student perceptions and stereotypes, and bring to the forefront difficulties and successes that staff members have experienced. Always leave the dialogue time with. "I can improve this by …"

7.   Establish a time for class meetings within the class. Often, students in high poverty do not have individuals to whom they can talk openly. Many times, in schools with a majority of low-income students, coping techniques must be taught and discussed. Additionally, in order to have a room of respect, class meetings should occur. I have observed meetings being used to discuss a class problem or to talk about student problems inside and outside the school. They can be very useful. If staff meetings are important, certainly class meetings are essential.

8.   Plan staff retreats, whether for a day or overnight. Time away together changes the level of dialogue and can provide a relationship-building experience. Teachers can use such opportunities to have discussions with other effective educators from the school. The technique can even be adapted to planning a class retreat within the classroom itself—I observed one effective educator in a high-poverty school bring a camping tent into the classroom, where a retreat was simulated

during the school day. The goal of this exercise was relationship-building and personal reflection, and it occurred once a year.

9. After observing a student or staff-member at work, leave a sticky note on his/her desk stating what you enjoyed seeing them learn or teach. Often, people become nervous and defensive when it is obvious that they are being observed. Many teachers will tell you that they can teach a great class all week, only to have the lesson fall apart when the principal enters the room, Either they become nervous, or the principal's presence causes the students' demeanor to change. Teachers should recognize that close observations of students can lead to the same result. This is really a perception and defensive disposition that occurs with observations. So, to calm the person you are observing and to build onto the positive relationship being developed, always mention something that you enjoyed watching, and leave that as an immediate feedback piece. If the lesson is a bad one, or if the student is unsuccessful at his or her task, the feedback may be very general.

10. Always inform students of their grades and the skills they need to improve. This can be done within the content you may want to stress. Too often, we make the mistake of telling only the parent how the student is doing, even when we know that the parent is unlikely to become involved in improving the student's work habits. Parent conferences can be helpful, but they are not tools to change learning in the classroom. Student conferences will have a much greater impact. Similarly, administrators should have ongoing assessment conferences with staff using data as well.

11. Administrators should assess staff regularly to measure growth and use specific areas in which to judge performance. In addition to evaluations, my staff was assessed on a rubric scale in various areas. The more feedback, the better. A good rule is to give feedback on observations within twenty-four hours if the feedback is going to affect the teaching process.

12. Create appropriate social opportunities within the school environment to reinforce staff relationships. At the school where I was principal, the staff had breakfast together every Friday. Teachers of particular grade-levels took turns hosting the breakfasts, which we held in the library forty minutes before school began.

13. Teachers should always make descriptive comments on every child's report card. Principals who make good instructional strides in their building read every report card, give staff feedback to ensure that they have a handle on students who are not succeeding, and identify patterns in certain classrooms. This also lets staff know that the principal takes the time to read about the progress of their students.

14. Do not allow any interruptions when you are meeting with a student, parent, or teacher. This should always be an important, protected, uninterrupted time. Principals who are constantly interrupted when they are in a conference with a student, teacher, or parent give the message that other things come first and are more important.

15. Be consistent in your expectations of student behavior when they enter the classroom. For example, let them know clearly that they are to come in, sit down, and copy a sentence. Good teachers have students who know exactly what to do when they arrive.

# CHAPTER 2

# QUESTIONING

Teach students how to question and how to incorporate the question in their responses.

Strategies

16.  Have students develop questions for adults and students about lessons or in book talks. I have seen effective teachers use this technique in book talks. After the class has read a book, a student leader will ask the students about it and will lead the discussion. The other students will then rate the leader on the quality of his or her questions.

17.  Teachers should use problem-solving lessons, in which they ask students to identify what information is missing before they can solve the problem.

18.  Teach students to ask themselves why an answer is correct and to include this reasoning in their response. "The answer is ____ because ____."

19. On worksheets, students should write down each step in the answer process, why the step is necessary, and the effect the step will have. This is especially useful in science and math.

20. Teach students the scientific method, and show them how to apply it in every content area. This is also referred to as "inquiry-based learning." Students should make an educated guess based on the information and data they have, test the educated guess using data and real facts, and draw a conclusion.

21. Inquiry-based learning is also a good tool to use with staff because, in high poverty schools, educators too often blame outside forces for the lack of learning. Asking them to identify a problem, make an educated guess as to its solution, testing this solution with data, and drawing a conclusion constitutes a simple way to give staff a good dose of reality. This will save schools lots of time and permit them to implement strategies that really solve problems. One school I worked in as a consultant was wasting time on strategies directed at improving the attendance of its poorest students. Once they used the method of inquiry outlined above, administrators realized that their poor students were not the ones missing the most school—it was, in fact, the higher-income kids.

22. Teach kids the game Twenty Questions. In this game, students have to guess an item in less than twenty questions. The better the questions, the fewer of them they will need to identify the object. This game can be used creatively for virtually any subject.

23. Teach students to ask "Why?", to ask it often, and to find the answers to their questions. Teachers can model this by regularly asking students similar questions. "Why? How do you know? Where did you learn that?"

24. As a class rule, when responding in writing or orally, students must always incorporate part of the question in their response. This will keep them focused on answering the question. This format is also a useful tool for test-taking.

# CHAPTER 3

# TEACHING LISTENING SKILLS

Most observers think that students are listening when they are quiet and looking at the instructor. In fact, they are often just hearing and watching, not listening. Think of the number of times that you believed you had taught a lesson well—everyone was quietly watching you—only to have, when the lesson was over, a student ask what he or she was supposed to do. The teacher's automatic response to this is often, "You were not listening." You should understand that the brain is four times faster in processing information than in formulating speech, which makes it difficult for listeners to maintain attention. (Schwartz 1999)

Strategies

25. Tell students that they will have listening activities in a series of mini-lessons. Read them a paragraph, and have them summarize what has been said by picking out the main points. The more often they do this, the more naturally they will be able to create an internal outline.

26. Ask students to summarize in a single phrase what you have stated, so as to reinforce their focus on the main point and comprehension.

27. After someone speaks, have the class develop key questions about what they have said. Have peers evaluate the questions by determining whether they ask for more information or simply re-ask something that was already stated. Does the question show that the person was listening? Is it related to the topic? Students can share their evaluations and defend them.

28. Have a listening center in the room, where students can review many different exercises.

29. Give students multi-step directions and evaluate how well they follow them, and therefore how well they have listened.

30. Quiz students weekly. Teach them to identify key words in questions, to find these words in the passage, to underline them, and to find the answers in that area of the text. For example, if the question is "What did he find in the snow?", the answer will be somewhere in the passage around the word "snow." Poor readers will try to read the entire passage, comprehend it, and then find the answer, which results in them either running out of time or forgetting what the question was.

31. Show students how to outline spoken information. This is a good way for notes to be taken instead of writing everything down and helps students learn to identify the main ideas in a lecture.

32. Have students routinely use the technique of listening to a story or conversation and identifying the central problem or main parts of the story. Often, high-poverty students get overwhelmed by details and lose the "big picture" thoughts. This technique helps them to practice listening and focusing on the main idea.

# CHAPTER 4

# INCORPORATING MORE READING AND WRITING

Reading and writing are the foundation for all other subjects. Students can be good in math, but if they can't read, they can't solve problems that aren't expressed in numerals alone. Reading and writing are indicators of success. Reading and writing work together. Students read like they write, and they write like they read. If a proper foundation is not laid early, students will often struggle in all other subjects as a result. It is imperative to teach reading and writing skills early on. However, even if students do not have these skills in later grades, it is possible to teach patterns and phonics in order to help them catch up quickly—and ultimately to help them perform better.

Strategies

33. Incorporate test vocabulary words in daily lessons. Teach students at least one new tested vocabulary word every day. Spell the word, define it, and use it. Post the words once they are taught.

34. Require students to use test vocabulary words in their writing. Post a list, or give students a book of tested vocabulary from which to select words. This will make them comfortable with using vocabulary that is commonly seen on tests.

35. Have students critique other books, determine whether they are well written, explain why or why not, and defend their critique with specifics. This will make them better writers.

36  Prediction skills can help students, both in school and elsewhere, to gain insight into other people's behavior. Have your students predict behavior throughout a book they are studying, citing specific reasons to support their predictions. In addition, at the end of a book, have students go back and find the hints that would have suggested the book's final outcome to them. Good authors tend to use hints and foreshadowing throughout their books.

37. Have students write on topics of interest daily. This can be done through journaling, by using a newspaper to select a topic to write on, or by allowing students to simply write creatively.

38. Have students critique and score their writing and that of their peers in a respectful format. Final writing pieces can be displayed on an overhead with a rubric or set of things to look for beside it. As a lesson, read, edit, and score the writing along with the class.

39. Teach students to identify the main point of a piece of writing. Mastering this skill will improve their scores in standardized testing. Teach students to read the questions first, then read the passage for the answer, concentrating on each sentence. They should disregard any sentence that does not answer the question. Ninety percent of tested reading materials consist of outside details. Students must learn to find the important 10 percent. Practice this technique regularly in class reading assignments.

40. Teach students to look at pictures, quickly identify what doesn't belong, and explain just as quickly how they eliminated outside factors.

41. Have students create questions about a text that focus on its main point.

42. Listen to speakers and have students outline their message while focusing on their main point. Evaluate the outlines.

43. Create tests in the format of the formal test, and have students take them weekly.

44. Have students practice writing on demand, like they must do when taking a standardized test. Teach the essential components students need to know when writing a piece. Teach proper writing procedure.

45. Use phonics within lessons, and allow students to study phonemic patterns for categories of words they have difficulty reading. Older children who can't read often fall behind by not catching on quickly enough to phonics. When they are passed on and no one works with them at home, they get farther and farther behind. Identify categories of words they don't know by having them read to you. Make a recording of their reading, and later play it back to yourself to determine whether they know blends, ending sounds, silent-letter patterns, and so on.

46 Have students listen to themselves read on tape and try to determine their own goals. Have them track their own improvement.

47. Have students read a variety of literature—magazines, newspapers, trade books, etc. Allowing them to read high-interest materials will create a greater desire in them to read and will familiarize them with different types of text.

48. Allow students to listen to books on tape and check them out for home use if they desire. Most often, students will return the materials

if an environment of respect has been established. Books on tape are particularly useful on the school bus.

49. Have students practice daily using word flash-cards. Good readers may use more difficult words than the lower-level readers, but this is a reading tool for everyone.

50. Have students, as a daily activity, break down words into phonetic parts and sound them out.

51. Require all students to respond to written questions in complete sentences.

52. Read to students daily. No matter what age group, all young people love to hear a good story. To hear something read aloud also serves to remind them of the proper tone and fluency of a good reading voice. You can read poems, short stories, or chapter books (reading a chapter a day).

53. Keep a "word wall" posted, and require students use these words in their writing.

54. Provide a dictionary to every student. When they are unsure of a word's meaning, ask them to look it up.

55. Establish book groups in which students read books at their level. You should then interact with the group in a book-talk fashion. Establish writing activities, math problems, and other activities that build on the reading material.

56. Have students publish their own writing, and understand the details of publishing, editing, copyrighting. Incorporate different genres (resource books, fiction, non-fiction, poetry) into this exercise.

57. Read about authors who started from humble beginnings. Teach students about individuals much like themselves who succeeded despite their circumstances. This establishes hope in students.

# CHAPTER 5

# ESTABLISHING A POSITIVE CLIMATE IN YOUR CLASS

Understand the mood of your students before the day starts, and establish a mood for them when they walk through the door. This will help head off problems during the day and will help students forget what the night before may have been like.

Strategies

58. Have students fill in the sentence, "I feel _____," or "I am _____." Then have them write five sentences about their statement. This can be done first thing in the morning, so as to allow them to get any problems off their minds.

59. I have seen teachers symbolically use a feather duster in low-income schools. As students walk through the doorway, they "dust" all the bad things away from them into an adjacent trash can, and the teacher gives them a hug.

60. Always greet your students at the door with a smile and a hello.

61. Keep snacks available or establish a relationship with the school nurse so that, when students start the day hungry, they can get a snack to settle their stomachs before lunch.

62. Tell your students when they first enter how excited you are to see them. When stated with sincerity, this goes a long way with students.

63. Establish a procedure within your class for when a student needs to see the school counselor or a social worker. Often teachers simply say, "Tell me if you need to talk with a counselor or a social worker," but this is not enough. Many students will not ask a teacher outright for the resource, but they will use it if it is made readily available. I have seen some teachers ask a school counselor to the classroom. If a student needed to see someone, they put their name on a card into that staff member's card pocket. When the teacher pulled the card, she scheduled time for the student with that staff person, no questions asked. Students must be taught how to use the system without abusing it.

64. Have the counselor or social worker stop by and check in with you regularly. Give lessons weekly or monthly within your classroom on topics your students deal with.

65. Keep a locked note-box on your desk where students can deposit personal notes for you regarding personal problems they might have. Teachers have told me that students have used this system to share issues they were dealing with in school and out of school. Peer-pressure issues have been settled within high-school classrooms using this method.

66. Make informal lunch-dates with your students. During the lunch-date, talk about what their previous evening was like. Discuss how their day is going, and allow them to lead the conversation in any direction they like.

# CHAPTER 6

# BEHAVIOR MODIFICATION AND CONSEQUENCES

According to Ruby Payne (2003), 5 percent of students create 90 percent of behavioral problems in the classroom. In addition, 8 percent of referrals and 80 percent of your difficulties with staff come from 11 percent of staff. The following strategies can be applied to students, and many of them to staff as well. Rather than talking about managing behaviors, the following strategies emphasize a basic structure for behavior modification.

Strategies

67. Be fearless. Do not show fear to students, parents, or other teachers if you want respect. High-poverty environments require a survival instinct. Many children are forced to prove their strength in different ways. This same proving of oneself continues into the classroom. If a student or parent knows that you are scared of them, they will not listen to you or respect you. In time, if you force yourself to appear fearless from the beginning less and less will seem frightening to you.

Remember that you cannot teach or discipline individuals of whom you are afraid.

68. Create consequences that suit the infraction. Discipline is really an opportunity to teach what is right. Punishing without teaching is a waste of time, and often the same behavior will recur if a student doesn't truly understand why it is wrong. Even though we feel that students know right from wrong—they know not to use foul language, they know that they shouldn't deface school property—we must still teach them a different way to behave while we are punishing them. For example, if a child writes foul language on a hall bulletin-board, instead of just punishing him or her with a detention, have the student maintain the bulletin-boards for a period of time, as a form of community service. The student then learns the hard work and time that is put into the boards and gains a kind of respect for them. If a child uses foul language during detention, require them to look up words in a dictionary or thesaurus that they could use instead, and have them list these new words. Another detention activity might be for students to research and write a paper on a writer who has used the power of words in a way that changed people for the better.

69. Compare the school to the real world whenever there is the opportunity. I have held "court sessions" in class when someone has been "charged" with a crime such as stealing or bullying. Lawyers are assigned, a jury of peers listens to the case, and a verdict is rendered. Students should understand real-world systems before they experience them for themselves. I often tell students and parents that school is the child's job, and if they break the rules, come late, or unprepared they will get "docked" or "fired," which may take the form of detention or in-school suspension. Another tactic is to explain that there are no good reasons for breaking rules. When a rule is broken in the real world, people go to jail. The police often don't question why you have broken one of society's rules or what might have led you to commit a crime. Societal terminology is good for students to hear, know, and be able to use.

# CHAPTER 7

# SETTING HIGH EXPECTATIONS

Ruby Payne (2003) cites a startling statistic in her research: 70 percent of special-education students come from poor backgrounds, and 70 percent of prisoners come from poor backgrounds as well. This can be interpreted as meaning that if we don't have high expectations of our young people and teach them how to survive properly, they will survive the only way they know how.

A good example of the power of one teacher was shared with me by my husband. He grew up in Tennessee in a very poor family with many siblings, and he had a wide variety of educational experiences in the Memphis City Public Schools. I now marvel at his brilliance and his ability to converse intelligently on any topic or subject. When we started dating in college many years ago, he told me that early on, in elementary school, he had a long line of teachers whose incompetence fed his low self-esteem. He had difficulties in reading and writing, and even in speaking, as he had a profound stuttering problem. It was not until he ended his elementary-school experience that a teacher sat him down and said to him, "Son, you have been overlooked."

Without realizing the impact this teacher would soon have on his life, he began looking forward to this teacher's class. He remembers this teacher spending time teaching him the basics and helping him catch up with his peers. He soon had not only caught up to them, but passed them. His language skills and vocabulary grew tremendously under this teacher's direction. He began to clearly articulate his thoughts verbally and in writing. The stuttering problem that had caused others to ridicule him dissipated and was replaced with correct, complex grammatical structure and syntax. Words flowed from him as though he had always been a master of the English language. His language skills and growing talent for questioning and understanding concepts eventually enabled him to lead his school to victory in the state mock trial competition.

The attentions of one special teacher created a young man who became valedictorian of his high school class, received undergraduate and graduate degrees in molecular biology, and eventually became an MD in obstetrics and gynecology. My husband, Stanley, is now a practicing obstetric physician in a top hospital. His brilliance is balanced by his humility, and he expects the best from everyone at all times. He has achieved all of this because one teacher had high expectations. You have the power to remove barriers for your students with your expectations for them to achieve great things.

Strategies

70. Implement a "no excuses" belief system. At the start of any child's experience in your class, you should tell him or her that there are no excuses for failure. Your class or school is a no-fail atmosphere. Students must learn what they did wrong and do the task over correctly. If you don't teach them how to do things the right way, they will continue doing things the wrong way. Following through with this sets a high standard. The measure of good teaching is how well your students have learned. If a student fails, then you have failed to teach. This policy also helps you meet your own high standards of effective teaching. It also means that some students will need certain

concepts to be presented again in different ways, which requires good teaching!

71. Set realistic school goals, and measure improvements in relation both to where you started and to the state standards (your target). Identify long-range goals for your class and divide them into six-week increments. Identify what skills your students must master by a given date. Some students—those who begin the year not reading at all, for example—may have a unique set of goals set out for them, but you must identify these in writing along with the rest of your class's goals. You must focus on where you are taking your students, even if they don't all have the same short-term destination.

72. Have students participate in activities to build self-confidence. Have them measure their own progress. Students must know within content areas how they are doing relative to where they started. Teach students how to self-evaluate, because this will be a life-long tool. A form for this can be found in the appendix to this book.

73. For high progress, many effective teachers state that, for their students to score in the various advanced content areas, they need to know _____. The teachers use this year-end goal to break down the skills mastered by quarter and to track their own performance.

74. Hold students accountable. When they fail to complete an assignment, grade them accordingly, then require them to complete it by the end of the school day. Assignments must always be completed—points may be subtracted when they are not done on time, but they must always be done.

75. Teach students that they must learn the basics of the real world if they are to survive and succeed. Given that many students begin dropping out after the sixth grade, it is imperative that life lessons be taught prior to that. For example, if students are not in an environment where parents use a checkbook—instead, they use money orders, and check-cashing places instead of banks—they will not automatically know how to use these tools. You should consider it part of your job

to teach them. Every student, upon leaving elementary school, should have a basic understanding of how checkbooks, savings accounts, and budgets work. Lessons on these topics can be incorporated in a variety of ways within the school. I have used and observed classroom and school stores. (An activity for this is located in the appendix.) As a teacher, I had students track stocks as if they were investors. I had them compare a hundred-dollar pair of Nikes to a hundred-dollar purchase of Nike stock and evaluate the relative value of each over time. This both empowered economically disadvantaged students with economic knowledge and began to transform some of their misplaced values regarding material goods. By the time they had completed this exercise, overpriced Nike shoes had become far less appealing to them.

# CHAPTER 8

# INCREASING PARENTAL INVOLVEMENT IN HIGH-POVERTY SCHOOLS

Parental involvement should not consist merely of attending a parent conference once or twice a year. For a parent to be involved is for him or her to be regularly engaged in the school's activities. The following strategies outline ways to involve parents.

Strategies

76. Identify parents who want to be involved. There is at least one parent per classroom who is willing to meet with the school. This core group will be the basis for a parent leadership team that can plan ways to engage other parents. Begin a dialogue with this group.

77. Identify needs within your community, and offer to host speakers on high-interest subjects. Obtain for parents resources and information regarding these subjects. We began offering information—after

PTO—on detecting lead levels, welfare to work, how to budget and stretch one's dollars, asthma-related services and resources, health fairs, and Medicaid enrollment opportunities. This is an excellent way to connect parents to your school.

78. When I was a principal, one strategy we used to get parents into our building daily was to place a washer and dryer on the lower level. While clothes washed and dried, parents visited their children's classrooms. They were allowed to do only one load of laundry per day, which resulted in a rotating presence of parents in the building at all times.

79. Identify parents with good skills that might be employed within the building. In high-poverty environments, unemployment is the most serious problem. If you have parents with good skills that are needed for jobs in the school, employ them! They will be the ones who recruit other parents when good things are happening in your building. When I was a principal, 10 percent of my school's staff consisted of parents.

80. Create a "phone tree." Assign particular parents a certain number of other parents to contact when the class is having a field trip or a school event that you would like parents to attend.

81. Keep parents updated through short, weekly newsletters.

82. When you want parents to attend an event, print the information on fluorescent sheets of paper that will grab their attention when the students bring them home.

83. Keep videos of class activities and school performances running in a high-parent-traffic area. This will pique their interest in events and show them what they have been missing.

84. When a child has participated in an event that a parent has missed, send a follow-up note home stating how great their child was, that you are sorry that they couldn't attend, and that you hope to see them next time.

85. Offer parent-education classes on the GED, Job Searching, Resume Writing, and related topics at your school.

86. Suggest easy ways for parents to work with their children at home, using daily household tasks. (A list of possibilities appears in the appendix.)

87. Send home or distribute at parent meetings lists of free services in the community. Parent might not ask for them, so make resources easy to access.

88. Humbly speak with and write to parents without using educational jargon. It is a big turn-off to many parents who are less educated when they cannot understand the teacher's message or when they feel that they are being condescended to. Parents are not likely to ask what you mean by something they don't understand, and so it is up to you to talk in a way that is easy for a non-educator to understand.

89. Call parents or send notes when their children do good things. This demonstrates care and concern on your part.

90. Give parents at least two weeks' advance notice of functions. Working parents do not always have the freedom to miss work or take a vacation day. If you want them to come to the school, they may have to request a change in their work schedule. Work schedules are usually made weekly or biweekly, so inform parents early if you want them to attend a function or an event.

91. Establish a parent room or area where parents can go to talk with their children, talk with other parents, have coffee, read about school events on a bulletin board, get extra school-lunch or health forms, and so on. I have seen a "parent corner" that was a rocking-chair in a hall corner enclosed by a parent bulletin board, a small selection of children's books, and free parenting magazines. I have also seen a dedicated room for parents containing a coffee pot, some parent resource materials for free, and some in a locked glass cabinet for

check-out. What works in your school will depend on its individual climate.

92. At every school performance, distribute lists of parent meeting dates and minutes, or print them on the back of the event program.

93  Have a teacher teach a fifteen-minute at-home school-support strategy at every PTO. Our teachers at the school where I was principal rotated this responsibility by grade level. They taught homework strategies, spelling activities, and even in-car word games. Give out any materials parents might need to implement these strategies.

94. Incorporate a "make it and take it" into PTO.

95. Develop a sense of urgency in parents regarding their children's future. Give them easy-to-understand data about student performance. Tell them about high minority prison rates, the school's demographics, its achievement rate, and any other information you think they might find useful. However, if too much information is presented at once, or if it is too difficult to understand, you might lose the parents' attention; so try to keep it simple.

# CHAPTER 9

# RESOLVING CONFLICTS WITH CHARACTER

Children from high-poverty households are faced with real-life challenges of survival. Strength is often tested in their environment, and a "survival of the fittest" attitude can easily carry over into the schoolhouse. Children in these situations rarely learn conflict resolution on their own, and if it is not directly taught, they will not be able to use it successfully in tough situations. Many teachers believe that, through modeling, they teach children the fundamentals of resolving conflicts. This false notion explains why students can be respectful in the classroom but act horribly on the playground or school bus, out of the teacher's sight. They have not learned how to resolve conflicts with character.

Strategies

96. Teach students to understand (through talking and role playing) that it takes much more energy, strength, control, and time to solve a problem by talking, compromising, and using reason. Understanding

they can wield more power and strength through this technique will make them more eager to learn it.

97. Have students describe difficult situations that they may face, and have them role-play appropriate responses.

98. Incorporate character education into everyday lessons.

99. Discuss peer pressure and the impact it has on your students. Use writing assignments that involve answering questions like "If this happened to you, what would you do?" Discuss the various responses and identify the ones that would work.

100. Often, students respond in aggressive ways to show strength in front of peers. Confront this fact with students, and have them list ways in which they can still appear strong and yet won't get them into trouble or involve violence.

101. Don't undermine what high-poverty students have to do outside of school. Simply state that, in school, there are other choices. Help them develop these choices inside the school to resolve conflicts.

# CONCLUSION

It is my hope that these strategies are used, are adapted, and cause other strategies to develop. Stories of high-performing high-poverty schools and teachers, such as "The Marva Collins Story," exemplify the power of good teaching. Marva Collins showed that, with her own money, she could start a school in her Chicago house for those considered the worst students—the supposedly unteachable. Her students consistently outperformed their peers in the Chicago public-school system. Years later, her graduates demonstrated the impact of such excellence on their lives. There are many other such schools: Kennard Academy in St. Louis, Missouri; Chic School in Kansas City, Missouri; and Pine Lawn Elementary in Normandy, Missouri, to name only a few. High-performing high-poverty schools like these can be found in every big city. By realizing what is possible, we can encourage ourselves and others to aspire for so much more within one classroom.

During my tenure as principal at Clark Academy in St. Louis City, a local story reached the national news when one of my fourth-grade students, Rodney Mcalister, was mauled to death after class in the park across the street from the school. He had last been seen alive by his classmates who had been playing basketball in the park. Rodney's body was found the next morning by a passerby. Many children who grow up in high-poverty environments are confronted in their everyday lives by things many of us could not imagine—stray dogs on the streets, drugs on street corners, gangs, and crime are the norm for them. It was around the time of Rodney's death that I reentered the classroom and became a teacher and principal at the same time. One of my third-grade students shared this poem with me. She said that it was what she called a "real-life" poem.

## Life Doesn't Frighten Me
### by Maya Angelou

Shadows on the wall
Noises down the hall
Life doesn't frighten me at all
Bad dogs barking loud
Big ghosts in a cloud
Life doesn't frighten me at all.
Mean old Mother Goose
Lions on the loose
They don't frighten me at all
Dragons breathing flame
On my counterpane
That doesn't frighten me at all,
I go boo
Make them shoo
I make fun
Way they run
I won't cry
So they fly
I just smile
They go wild
Life doesn't frighten me at all.
Tough guys in a fight
All alone at night
Life doesn't frighten me at all.

Panthers in the park
Strangers in the dark
No, they don't frighten me at all.
That new classroom where
Boys pull my hair
(Kissy girls
With their hair in curls)
They don't frighten me at all.
Don't show me frogs and snakes
And listen for my scream,
If I'm afraid at all
It's only in my dreams.
I've got magic charm
That I keep up my sleeve,
I can walk the ocean floor
And never breathe.
Life doesn't frighten me at all
Not at all
Not at all.
Life doesn't frighten me at all.

# Appendix—Forms

**Developing Character**
**Read and Respond**

Read the situation below, and respond.

Norman is wearing a new pair of tennis shoes to school. They match the new clothes that he purchased with the money he earned from his after-school job. While Norman walks down the hall with his friends, Michael steps on Norman's shoes and leaves a large, muddy footprint on them. Michael keeps walking and doesn't look back. Norman's friends say, "Man, are you going to take that?"

Finish the response.

a. If Norman responds by grabbing Michael and hitting him …


b. How can Norman resolve this peacefully and feel good about the situation?

## Activity to Practice Prediction

Paste a picture (animal pictures work best) on the inside of a manila folder. Make cuts across the front flap of the folder so that different flaps can be pulled back to show different portions of the picture. Have students use details from the portions exposed to predict what the pictures portray.

| | Paste picture inside. |
|---|---|
| _____ | |
| _____ | |
| _____ | |
| _____ | |
| _____ | |
| _____ | |
| _____ | |
| _____ | |
| _____ | |
| Cut lines across front flap. | |

## Parent Letter for At-Home Skills

Dear Parent,

These are some things that you can do to reinforce basic school skills at home.

1. When driving or walking home, ask your child to estimate how long it will take to get home. Look at the time, and have them guess what time it will be when you get home. Older children can try to guess the number of miles.

2. Have your child cook and read measurements from recipes. Have them use 1 cup, 1 teaspoon, a ½ cup, and so on.

3. Talk to your child about their day, every day. Since some children don't like talking about their day with adults, start by asking your child to tell you three things they learned in class. If you just ask children what they did during the day, they will tend to say nothing. Asking them to tell you three specific things they learned lets them focus their minds better on their answer.

4. Allow your child to write your grocery list or to cross items off your list as you find them in the store.

5. Over the weekend, have your child write in a notebook about their day.

6. Turn your child's spelling words into flash cards that they can do each night.

7. Have your child draw on paper what the moon looks like at night and keep track of how it changes over the week.

8. Give your child multistep directions to do at home to help them practice listening to and following directions. For example: (1) Go to the kitchen and turn off the lights; (2) Get the book from my bedroom; and (3) Bring me my book and reading glasses.

9. Have your child listen to a weather report and determine whether it is going to be cold or hot, and what clothes that means they need for the next day.

10. Have your child put in order (by size or alphabet) items in a cabinet. This is excellent practice for sequencing skills.

## Checks and Balances

Congratulations! All students have been employed as workers. Their job is to be a good student by coming to work on time, being prepared to learn, being dressed appropriately, and completing good work. The rules for our world of work are below.

Classroom Company Name:_____

All students will start their day with a deposit of $5.00 each. In one week, everyone could have earned $25.00, less taxes.

We have stated the deposits. Now, for the deductions:

Taxes: 10 cents weekly

Chewing in class: _____.

Improper clothing, sagging clothes: _____.

Late assignments: _____.

No assignment: _____.

Other deductions: _____.

At the end of each day, you need to balance your checkbook. At the end of the month, there will be a class store where you can purchase goods with checks.

Student _____      Balance _____

| Check # | Date | Payable to | |
|---------|------|------------|---|
| | | | |
| | | | |

Student's Name _____      CHK #_____

Classroom _____

Pay to the order of _____      _____

Amount to be paid _____

Memo _____      Signature _____

## Developing Character
## Student Leader Leads a Class Meeting

Think about a topic you want to discuss. Write the topic here:_____.

List five points you want to be sure to discuss within your topic.

1.

2.

3.

4.

5.

Think about how you will start the discussion. Will you talk about a class problem? Will you use a newspaper story, magazine article, or picture for discussion? Will you concentrate on a good experience or discuss a book?

I will start leading the discussion by _____

_____

Points to remember

- Be fair in giving everyone a chance to talk and express their opinion.

- It is okay if the discussion goes in a different direction than you expected.

- Have fun!

**Taking a Look at My Own Work**

Name _____ Date _____

Assignment _____

My goals for this assignment are to

1.

2.

3.

| Poor | Good but could be better | Good | Excellent |
|---|---|---|---|
| My work was poor in the following ways … | My work could have been better by … | My work was good because … | |

I can improve my work by _____

_____

_____

| Goals | Circle one | Why |
|---|---|---|
| 1. | Goal was met.<br><br>Goal was not met. | |
| 2. | Goal was met.<br><br>Goal was not met. | |

KG-2 Form

## Taking a Look at My Own Work

Name _____ Date _____

Assignment _____

Check everything you think you did well

| | |
|---|---|
| I was neat. | |
| I took my time. | |
| I finished my work. | |
| I followed directions. | |
| The work was fun. | |
| Other areas (Teacher can add items below or have the student add items below specific to the assignment.) | |
| | |

Circle one.

My grade on this work should be a _____.

A                 B                 C

**Teacher-Student Interview Form**
**Student Interview Questions**

Student_____

Date_____

1.   What is your favorite activity at school?

2.   Who do you consider your friends at school and at home?

3.   What does it mean to be popular?

4.   Are you popular?

5.   What subjects are you smart in?

6.   Who disciplines you at home?

7.   What happens when you get in trouble?

8.   When you get home, who is there?

9.   Do you have brothers and sisters?

10.  Do you like school? Why or why not?

12.  If you could eat lunch with anyone, who would it be?

13.  What is one thing teachers do that you don't like?

# BIBLIOGRAPHY

Angelou, M. And Still I Rise Poems. New York: Random House, 1978.

Bell-Rose, S. What It Takes: A Look at Black Achievers. College Board Review, 187, 8–19. (1998–1999)

Covey, S. The Seven Habits of Highly Effective People. New York: Simon and Schuster, 1989.

Edmonds, R.R. School effects and teacher effects. Social Policy, 15(2), 37–39, 1984.

ERIC Clearinghouse on Urban Education. The Educational Policies and Practices Whose Effectiveness in Closing the Achievement Gap Has Been Shown, 2001.

Gardner, H. The Unschooled Mind: How Children Think and How Schools Should Teach. New York: Basic Books, 1991.

Grissmer, D., & Flanagan, A. Exploring Rapid Achievement Gains in North Carolina and in Texas. Washington, DC: National Educational Goals Panel, 1998.

Heifetz, R. & Linsky, M. Leadership on the Line. Boston, MA: Harvard Business School Press, 2002.

Hilliard, A. Every Child Should Succeed. Video series.

Kozol, J. Savage Inequalities. New York: Harper Perennial, 1991.

Kunjufu, J. Countering the Conspiracy to Destroy Black Boys, vol. 1. Chicago: African Images, 1984.

Leithwood, K. Editor's conclusion: What we learned and where we go from here? School effectiveness and school improvement, 3(2), 173–184, 1992.

Lickona, T. Educating for Character. New York: Bantam Books, 1989.

National Task Force on Minority High Achievement. Reaching the Top: A Report of the National Task Force on Minority High Achievement. New York: The College Board, 1999.

North Central Regional Educational Laboratory.

Payne, R. The Framework of Poverty. Highland, TX: Aha Process Inc.4, 2001.

Payne, R. Train the Trainers conference. Evansville, IN, 2003.

Ragland, M. A., Asera, R., & Johnson, J.F. Urgency, Responsibility, Efficacy: A Study of Nine High Performing, High Poverty Urban Elementary Schools. Austin, TX: Charles Dana Center, 1999.

Sadowski, Michael. Closing the Gap One School at a Time. Harvard Education Letter, 17(3), 1–3, 5, 2001.

Schwartz, W. Closing the Achievement Gap: Principles for Improving the Educational Success of All Students. ERIC Digest. New York, New York. ERIC Clearinghouse on Urban Education, 2001.

Saint Louis Public Schools. Clark School, St. Louis, MO, 2003.

Schwartz, E. How to Double Your Child's Grades in School. New York: Barnes and Noble Books, 1997.

Sekou, U. O. Urban Souls. St. Louis, MO: Urban Press, 2001.

Shaker Heights School District. Shaker Heights High School, Shaker Heights, Ohio, 2003.

The Journal of Blacks in Higher Education. October 2004.

United States Census, 2003.

Viadero, D. "Setting the Bar: How High?" Education Week. XVII (17), 21–26, 1999.

Warren-Sams, B. Closing the Achievement Gap Requires Multiple Solutions. Northwest Regional Educational Laboratory, 1997.

Wong, Harry & Wong, Rosemary. The Effective Teacher video series. Harry K. Wong Publications.

978-0-595-33478-0
0-595-33478-4

Made in the USA
Lexington, KY
10 May 2010